Jesus

or

Yeshua?

Exploring the Jewish Roots
of Christianity

Louis Lapides

Jesus or Yeshua: Exploring the Jewish Roots of Christianity

Printed in the United States of America
ISBN: 9780615678771

Learn more information at:
www.scripturesolutions.com

scripture
SOLUTIONS

Table of Contents

Section 1
Initial Thoughts

Here's a shocker . . . Jewish people don't feel at ease in a Christian church. The first time I attended a Protestant congregation, a Southern Baptist one, I couldn't avert my eyes from the 10-foot tall stained glass mosaic of Jesus looming behind the pastor. I imagined for a few moments the man from Galilee was about to step out of the window, float over to my pew and ask whether I noticed the "Jews Not Welcome" sign at the church's front door. "Of course," I would respond, "But Jesus, aren't you ...?"

Upon further reflection I figured out why I experienced the heebie-jeebies on my initial visit. As a Jewish seeker of truth, I was convinced I was cheating on the God of Israel. Why did worshipping in a Gentile Christian church make me feel like I was unfaithful? Was I cheating on my Bar Mitzvah? Was I betraying Abraham or Moses?

Was it the pastor's perfectly pressed suit and tie graced by his Southern Baptist grin? It could have been the Sunday morning promise of that evening's Lord's Supper that did not turn out to be the smorgasbord I anticipated. I left the service feeling spiritually fulfilled; however, I was famished.

I slowly discovered my discomfort stemmed from the culturally alien environment of a Gentile church. I couldn't blame them. It wasn't their fault they were not Jewish. Yet it didn't feel like I was at Temple Bnai Abraham, the house of worship I attended as a child in Newark, New Jersey.

Each time I entered a church building all I could see were crosses, wall-to-wall beaming Gentiles and hearing the words "Christ" and "Christian" sprinkled into every conversation. I later heard that such church-talk is labeled "Christianeze," and all Christians learn the lingo quite quickly.

I did not fit. Church did not feel Jewish. The jargon was not Jewish. The terminology caused me to cringe, asking, "What have I gotten myself into?" When the pastor referred to me as a *Baptist kid*, I knew it was time to delve deeper into this Christian faith that was launched 2000 years ago by courageous Jewish followers of Jesus. I needed to know what happened to a messianic movement started in Israel that now feels more like it was birthed in Nashville, Tennessee (and I happen to love Nashville and its music).

How did the Church navigate itself from the Jewish customs of first century Jerusalem to eating ham when celebrating Easter Sunday? Historically, the twelve disciples were enjoying a Passover Seder complete with Matzah, bitter herbs and lamb prior to the death, burial and resurrection of Jesus. In contrast, I can't fathom how ham sneaked into the traditional celebratory meal most Christians enjoy on Resurrection Day (Easter). Don't get me wrong. I have nothing against a ham and Swiss cheese sandwich on rye with a smear of spicy deli mustard. But gorging on a pig to commemorate the resurrection of Israel's long-awaited Messiah?

I understood a good place to start to recapture the Jewishness of Christianity is its terminology and definitions. Language can create a whole new atmosphere especially in a religious setting.

Section 2
Why Sound "Jewish" in a Christian Church?

Three reasons stand out for using language that is sensitive to the Jewish roots of the New Testament faith:

1. *To help Jewish people understand that belief in the Messiah is harmonious with being Jewish.* If Jewish or Gentile people who follow Jesus (Yeshua) unthinkingly use undefined Christian terms in the presence of Jewish people who don't believe in Jesus, we create a perception of detachment from the Jewishness of Christianity.

Consistency is essential. If we as messianic Jews claim it is Jewish to believe in Jesus, and our children observe us embrace a lifestyle missing Jewish cultural forms and vernacular, the next generation will be confused. Though the Jewish community directs the charge of deception at Jewish followers of Jesus for "dressing Christianity up in Jewish garb," they mistakenly sidestep the Jewish origins of the New Covenant faith.

2. *To expose the "excess baggage" of traditional Christian cultural influences on the messianic faith.* Restoring Jewishness to Christianity is not bringing an unfamiliar element into the historical Christian faith, but exposing the foreign influence of Gentile culture that has replaced the Hebrew roots of our messianic faith.

Jewish lifestyle was the culture and expression of the New Testament faith in its earliest stages. In the New Testament Acts 21:20 informs us Jewish believers did not jettison their connection to their Hebraic identity, "When they heard this, they praised God. Then they said to Paul: 'You see, brother, how many thousands of Jews have believed, and all of them are zealous for the law'" (New International Version, NIV, unless otherwise noted all scripture citations in this work are referenced from the NIV).

Unfortunately, the Jewish expression of faith in Jesus was shrouded and lost in later Christian history. No wonder Acts 12:4 reads in the King James Version (KJV), "And when he had apprehended him [Paul], he put him in prison, and delivered him to four quaternions of soldiers to keep him; intending after *Easter* (author's italics) to bring him forth to the people." The expression *Easter* is not in the Greek text, but rather the word *pascha* which should be translated into English as "Passover."

In 1611, the translators of the KJV had imposed the third century observance of Easter into the first century text of the New Testament, thus removing the Jewish historical background from the messianic faith.

Gentile cultural practices such as Easter and Christmas were never part of early Christianity, though they are useful and appropriate celebrations today.

Currently, New Testament believers can observe Resurrection Day as an opportunity to celebrate the new life we have in the Messiah. Concerning the Christian's link to the resurrection of Yeshua, Paul writes, "If we have been united with Him like this in His death, we will certainly also be united with Him in His resurrection" (Romans 6:5).

The same can be said regarding Christmas. Many Jewish and Gentile followers of Jesus focus on the pagan origins of Christmas and reject the holiday outright. Consequently, they often judge those who celebrate the birth of the Messiah and use secular traditions such as Christmas trees, exchanging gifts and Christmas decorations. In contrast, I find Christmas as a wonderful opportunity to declare our faith in the incarnation of the Son of God.

Many practices found in Christmas celebrations are not rooted in the Scriptures. Yet many traditions in Jewish celebrations have no foundation in the Torah as well such as giving gifts on the eight days of Hanukkah or wearing costumes depicting the characters in the Book of Esther on Purim. To those believers who make a big deal out of these "holiday issues," I want to say, "Get a life!"

The messianic Jewish perspective should not question the existence of Gentile Christian festivals as ways to express Christian tradition; the only issue is the intentional historical removal of the Jewish underpinning from Christianity in an attempt to strip faith in Jesus from its Jewish origins.

3. *To invite Christians to enjoy the rich Jewish heritage of their spiritual roots.* In order for Christians to connect to the Hebraic roots of New Testament Christianity, it is helpful to include some messianic terminology within evangelical congregations. You'll notice I advocate "some." It would be foolish to have Gentile dominated churches speaking so much messianic lingo that the environment feels more like a synagogue than a building containing non-Jewish worshippers of Christ.

When a Jewish seeker of New Covenant truth enters a church where he observes the celebration of Passover and hears the Hebrew blessings cited over the bread and wine at the Lord's Supper, that person is made to feel at home. Feeling accepted, he is able to hear the message of salvation through Jesus without stumbling over cultural barriers inherent in a Christian subculture.

Section 3
Your First Exposure to Messianic Fluency

The first rule of thumb is not to fall apart if you forget to use a messianic term and default to the traditional Christian lingo. However, it is a good idea to introduce some of the following messianic terms into your everyday speech about your faith.

Yeshua

Rather than use the name "Jesus," *Yeshua* is a better expression to communicate the Jewishness of the Messiah. *Yeshua* is from the Hebrew root *Yasha* "to save." Thus, the name *Jesus* means "the salvation of the Lord" as reflected in Matthew 1:21, "You shall call His name Jesus [Yeshua] because He shall save His people from their sins."

The Hebrew name *Yeshua* has been translated into Greek as "Yesus" and then carried into English as *Jesus*. There is nothing superior about the English name *Jesus* as opposed to its Greek or Hebrew equivalent. *Yeshua* was the name the Messiah employed while He lived on earth, and it was the designation He heard His parents, brothers and sisters as well as His disciples call Him throughout His life.

Sadly, thousands of Jewish people have been persecuted during the dark periods of church history **in the name of Jesus** so this designation bears some stigma. The term *Yeshua* communicates Jesus as the Messiah for both Jewish people and Gentiles. Our goal is to make sure when Jewish people hear the name of the Lord, they associate His name with the gift of salvation and not the past dark history of misguided Christian persecution of Jewish people.

It is important to note that throughout this booklet I use *Yeshua* and *Jesus* interchangeably. I assume I am speaking to a mixed readership of Jewish and Gentile people. Consequently, I feel the freedom to use both terms as a matter of writing style. When I am in a predominately Jewish audience hostile to the gospel or indifferent, I will use "Yeshua" exclusively.

If I am addressing a largely Gentile assembly, I will not keep referring to Jesus as "Yeshua" since that is not part of their heritage. I believe we have a lot of freedom in this area. We need to be cautious about condemning Christians who fail to use "Yeshua" at all. We also need to be careful to not create a messianic congregational setting where mentioning the name of "Jesus" becomes a mortal sin.

Messiah

Instead of the title *Christ*, a person can use *Messiah*. When I first heard the gospel message, I was asked, "Who is Jesus Christ?" I responded in all seriousness, "He was the son of Joseph and Mary Christ." I was unaware that *Messiah* comes from the Hebrew word *Mashiach* which means, "anointed one," and in the Greek is translated *Messias* or the English *Messiah*. *Christ* actually comes from the Greek word *Christos* meaning, "anointed one".

The name *Christ* has taken on a non-Jewish and sometimes anti-Jewish connotation in the minds of many Jewish people. Using the Hebraic term *Messiah* rather than *Christ* stresses the fact *Yeshua* came as the Messiah to Israel and not *exclusively* for the Gentile nations.

Believer

Rather than use the well-worn term *Christian*, the word *believer* communicates a more positive message. To some Jewish minds, Christians are people who have hated and oppressed Jews for centuries.

Though *Christian* is a great word to describe what New Testament believers stand for, it has become specifically and exclusively employed as a reference to Gentile believers. In contrast, 1 Peter

4:16 in the New Testament employs the phrase to designate both Jewish and Gentile followers of Israel's Messiah, "However, if you suffer as a *Christian* (author's italics), do not be ashamed, but praise God that you bear that name."

Christian comes from the Greek *Christianos*, which means "those who belong to the Messiah." The word *Christian* is used only three times in the New Covenant (Acts 11:26; 26:28; 1 Peter 4:16). It is sometimes a detriment to a clear presentation of the Gospel that one term used only three times in the Scriptures now categorizes all followers of the Messiah.

Furthermore, the name *Christian* has become synonymous with Gentile cultural expressions so the Jewish person assumes that to become a Christian, he or she is trading in a corned beef sandwich on rye for a ham sandwich on white bread smothered in mayonnaise.

Other terms used in the New Covenant to describe followers of Yeshua are *believers* (Acts 10:45;1 Thessalonians 1:7; 1 Timothy 6:2) and *disciples* (Matthew 5:1; 8:1; 9:19). The term *believer* focuses on a person's commitment or trust to follow the Lord Jesus and not on one's ethnicity.

Despite the tendency of Christians to employ *believer* to describe themselves, the words *disciple* or *disciples* are used a total of 240 times in the Gospels and the Book of Acts. In Acts 2:14 and 19:23 adherents to the messianic faith are called "followers of the Way."

In summary, the follower of Jesus has a variety of terms to use to describe himself other than *Christian*.

Messianic

This phrase is a more recent reference to believers involved in messianic congregations. *Messianic* is actually an equivalent term to *Christian* since both include the word *Messiah* or *Christ*. When applied to Jewish followers of Yeshua, one is simply identifying believers in Jesus who are of Jewish descent. When we use *messianic*, we refer to that expression of the New Covenant faith that expresses itself in a Jewish manner.

Congregation

Although *messianic congregations* are not traditionally called "churches," they still function as churches or New Testament fellowships. To the Jewish mind, churches are associated with the loss of cultural, religious and social Jewish identity- in other words, everything that is not Jewish.

Growing up in a conservative Jewish home, I concluded church was a place filled with statues of saints, strangely garbed religious personnel, candles, crosses tainted with blood and thorns and stained glass windows with pictures of a stereotypical fair-haired, blue-eyed Jesus.

How do we understand the word *church* in a biblical context? *Church* is derived from the Greek *ekklesia* which can be defined as "called-out ones." An *ekklesia* is a "called out gathering of people." It is translated from the Hebrew word *Kahal* which means, "to call." In the Greek Old Testament (Septuagint) the words used to translate *kahal* are *sunagoge* and *ekklesia*. Both words refer to a "gathering of people." Thus, the term *congregation* or *assembly* is a more accurate way to translate *ekklesia* as a body of people who gather to worship Jesus as Messiah and Lord. (For further discussion on the meaning and usage of the word *Church* see Robert L. Saucy's book, *The Church in God's Program* [Moody Press, 1972] pp. 11-18).

Messianic Congregation

A *messianic congregation* is a local assembly of Jewish and Gentile believers in Jesus who gather for the purposes of worship, instruction in God's word, fellowship, outreach, accountability, baptism, the Lord's Supper and the exercise of spiritual gifts.

In a sense, messianic congregations should be like any other Christian house of worship in that they function as a New

Testament congregation. However, messianic congregations have unique and specific emphases in contrast to the broader Body of Messiah: expressing Jewish cultural forms at regular worship services; observing the feasts and holidays of Israel in a biblical and Messiah centered manner; identifying with the Jewish people at large; rekindling the understanding of the inherent Hebrew roots of Old and New Testament faith in Yeshua; maintaining the New Testament Gospel priority to the Jew first and also to the Gentile (Romans 1:16) and maintaining a messianic Jewish remnant as a witness to God's faithfulness to Israel (Romans 11:1-6).

Section 4
Touchy Terms in a Messianic Congregation

A number of normally accepted and beloved evangelical terms often cause Jewish seekers to balk and feel estranged from a faith that is rooted in their own tradition. It behooves Christians to know these "hot" buttons and be sensitive to expressions that can become turn offs to individuals who are sincerely asking meaningful questions about New Testament revelation.

Conversion

To Jewish people, the phrase *conversion* implies turning away from their Hebraic identity and embracing Gentile culture. Biblically, "conversion" speaks of turning to God and not to any specific culture - Jewish or non-Jewish. Psalm 51:13 states: "Then I will teach transgressors your ways, and sinners will turn back to you." Psalm 19:7 relates, "The law of the LORD is perfect, reviving the soul." In both passages the words *turn back* and *reviving* stem from the Hebrew *shuv* "to turn back, return." The KJV uses the phrase "convert" in both passages. Consequently, to *convert* is to turn back to God and repent.

Conversion in a biblical context has little to do with a change of ethnic background, but the focus is on a change of direction in life. A converted person is one who no longer backs away from God, hiding his sin, but moves towards the Lord's presence in confession of sins, repentance and finding forgiveness of his transgressions by confessing Jesus as Redeemer. If a believer chooses to use the word *convert* in the presence of a Jewish individual, it would be a wise choice to provide the biblical background of the word.

17

Baptism

Unless a Jewish individual has a grasp of the biblical background of *baptism*, this rite can be a deal breaker when it comes to deciding whether or not to accept Jesus. Some Jewish believers, who decide to follow their Messiah, slam on the brakes when it comes to taking the "plunge."

Jewish parents have told their messianic children, "We can accept that you believe in Jesus, just as long as you don't get baptized." To the Gentile believer, this dialogue seems strange. Perhaps some explanation would help to clarify this major stumbling block to the Jewish mind.

Historically, *baptism* has been associated with forced conversion in the Middle Ages when unsaved Jewish people were compelled to be baptized by so-called Christian clergy and crusaders in order to "save the Jewish soul." In the modern Jewish mind, "baptism" is considered a point of no return. Once baptized, the Jewish individual is lost to the people of Israel and is accused of turning his or her back on his Jewish heritage. He is a traitor.

Biblically, *immersion* or *baptism* is an external act in which the follower of the Lord deliberately signifies his or her *identification* with the Messiah Yeshua. It is an outward act that portrays the inward choice of accepting Jesus as Lord and Redeemer. *Baptism* and *immersion* symbolize the new birth experienced by followers of Yeshua.

Paul aptly explains this concept in his New Testament letter to a congregation in Rome, "We were therefore buried with him through baptism into death in order that, just as Christ [Messiah] was raised from the dead through the glory of the Father, we too may live a new life" (Romans 6:4).

Immersion does not save an individual, but provides an opportunity for the believer to act in obedience to the Lord's command to be immersed: "Therefore go and make disciples of all nations, baptizing them in the name of the Father and of the Son and of the Holy Spirit" (Matthew 28:19).

Immersion is analogous to a wedding ceremony. The external ritual of reciting vows and exchanging rings does not create the commitment of love necessary for marriage, but provides the couple with a public arena to declare the love they already share for one another. Immersion is a believer's public declaration of their choice to follow the Lord.

Evangelism

The word *outreach* is preferable. *Evangelism* broadcasts the connotation of Gospel revival meetings and crusades in which there have been covert attempts to "convert the Jews to Christ." Don't forget evangelism still carries negative baggage in light of recent scandals involving TV evangelists in the areas of morality, financial impropriety and religious fraud. The term *outreach* or *sharing one's faith* is less threatening to any sincere inquirer of the gospel message.

Evangelism and *proselytize* are buzzwords that often fill Jewish people with fear and cause them to proceed with caution when Christians attempt to befriend them. The Jewish person may question the Christian's motives and wonder, "Are you only befriending me so I join Christianity? Do you really care about me as a person or am I just a spiritual mark?"

In relation to both Jewish and Gentile people, our goal is to share the message of salvation in a friendly, intelligent manner – not to add pressure to accept Yeshua or trick them into making a profession of faith. The best approach in sharing the messianic faith is to simply speak about one's relationship with Jesus, articulate how He has transformed your life and respond to any objections a Jewish person might bring up. Be an example of how the Messiah changes a person's life.

Remember, you are not dependent on the cleverness of your presentation or arguments to convince a person of the truth of the gospel message. When sharing one's walk with the Lord, trust the Holy Spirit to deal with a seeker's heart and mind. You can always seek further answers to their questions and refer them to specific books dealing with their concerns.

Cross

Messianic congregations intentionally do not display the symbol of the cross. For many Jewish people, the cross —a symbol sacred to Christians — has become a historical representation of persecution in Jesus' name.

Obviously, contemporary Christians eschew any form of persecuting another faith in the name of Jesus. Yet, in a Jewish person's way of thinking, the roots of violence under the banner of the cross run deep – the Inquisitions, Crusades, pogroms and racism by so-called Christians. The sign of the cross remains a stumbling block to Jewish people, keeping them from hearing the true message of Jesus' death and resurrection.

As messianic believers, we prefer to focus on the redemptive message of the cross rather than its symbolic representation. However, in messages in which the cross is preached within the context of the Messiah's atonement for our sins, it is proper and necessary to use the word *cross*.

It is not necessary to use the awkward terms "tree" or "execution stake" to describe the instrument upon which Jesus died. To the Jewish mind, using these substitute terms for *cross* sound quite contrived.

Let me also say a word about Jewish believers who are ready to *plotz* if someone should say the word "cross" or display a crucifix. After several years of walking with the Lord, the believer should be mature enough to not allow the symbolism or the language describing Yeshua's death to cause them to become hysterical.

Some Jewish believers are so hyper-focused on their Jewish identity and messianic issues that they haven't the faintest idea of the importance of the cross to their spiritual lives. Rather than veiling or hiding the cross in a messianic congregation, it is essential that the message of the cross take center stage. It is my conviction that many messianic Jews remain in a state of spiritual immaturity because they have never truly approached the cross as sinners, repented of their sin and grasped the necessity of overcoming the power of sin through the presence of the Spirit of God.

The message we want to communicate through the use of the word *cross* is the offer of redemption through our Lord and Messiah Yeshua. Remember the gripping words of Paul, "I am not ashamed of the gospel, because it is the power of God for the salvation of everyone who believes: first for the Jew, then for the Gentile" (Romans 1:16).

Missionary/ Missions

To the seeking Jewish mind, using terms like *missionary* or *missions* is confusing and threatening. Unfortunately, verbiage in which mission organizations speak of "taking the world for Christ" remind a Jewish person of past crusades and mass efforts to compel Jewish people to convert to Christianity. Such phrases sound like a conspiracy to rid the world of religious pluralism and institute a society in which Christianity is the dominating faith to the exclusion of all others. Judaism does not appear to have a valid role in this futuristic Christian universe. Though the perception of this so-called Christian world is a knee-jerk reaction by Jewish people, such a vision—true or false—is a frightening prospect.

To communicate the Christian biblical commitment to *missions*, it is best to describe our calling as an *outreach* or *sharing of our faith* or bringing the messianic message to other people groups. Be creative! Most of all, be enthusiastic about the impact Christian workers in other countries are having among nationals. Rather than focus on the Christian goal to spread the word of God across the globe, pinpoint the results of changed lives in these cultures. Be able to list the relief efforts provided by different Christian outreach organizations that have helped victims of natural catastrophes.

Additionally, share how Christian medical missionaries are volunteering their expertise to treat disease, offer preventative medical treatment and perform life saving surgeries in the name of the Lord.

No one need be ashamed of the efforts of compassion displayed by both short and long term workers in foreign lands. Keep abreast of what is taking place throughout the world by reading magazines published by Christian organizations such as *Samaritan's Purse*, *Mercy Ships* and others describing their ministry efforts.

Communion

In messianic congregations, participants prefer the term *Lord's Supper* when describing communion. The words *communion* or *Eucharist* can sound high church and Roman Catholic, thus unintentionally stripping this ordinance of its Jewish roots in the Passover Seder. It is important that both Jewish people and Christians know Yeshua was observing Passover when He instituted what we commonly call the *Lord's Supper*.

In Matthew's account of the last Passover in Jesus' life, the text states in chapter 26:26-28, "While they were eating, Jesus took bread, gave thanks and broke it, and gave it to his disciples, saying, 'Take and eat; this is my body.' Then he took the cup, gave thanks and offered it to them, saying, 'Drink from it, all of you. This is my blood of the covenant, which is poured out for many for the forgiveness of sins. '"

To many Christians, Jesus and His disciples were eating a normal meal at which Jesus took a loaf of leavened bread or Italian roll, tore the bread in half and passed the remnants to the disciples. Actually, Jesus was partaking of the Passover (Matthew 26:19; Luke 22:7-8). He was not eating a loaf of normal white bread but unleavened bread or *matzah*. In addition, when the Lord blessed the bread and the wine, He offered the traditional Jewish prayers over the *matzah* and the cup of wine. The text in Matthew 26 says Jesus "gave thanks." He then customarily prayed the Jewish blessing, "Blessed art Thou, O Lord our God, King of the Universe, who has created the fruit of the vine."

In Matthew 26:30 the text reports, "When they had sung a hymn, they went out to the Mount of Olives." What was this hymn? Was it a gospel hymn like "The Old Rugged Cross" as appropriate as it would have been that moment? Rather, they sung a portion of the *Hallel*, the traditional Jewish hymn based on Psalm 118 repeated after the Passover meal.

It is highly recommended for Christians to deepen their appreciation and understanding of the Lord's Supper by attending a messianic Passover Seder. After all, according to Paul in I Corinthians 5:7-8 Jesus is our Passover Lamb, "For Christ, our Passover lamb, has been sacrificed. Therefore let us keep the Festival, not with the old bread leavened with malice and wickedness, but with the unleavened bread of sincerity and truth."

By reading through the Passover prayer book (the *Haggadah*), the Christian can learn how Jesus fulfilled the Passover feast through His sacrifice as the Passover Lamb of God.

Church

Though this term has been discussed previously, a few more comments are necessary. Christian history has provided the crayons that have colored the term "church" and has not painted a friendly portrait for Jewish people. The Christian who invites a Jewish person to their church has to understand the hesitancy often felt by them. The Christian sees his or her church as a place of spiritual refuge where God is honored, praise songs are lifted to the Lord in worship, the Word of God is taught and their deepest needs are met by a holy and loving Heavenly Father.

A Jewish person expects to enter a "church" seeing a bloodied Christ hanging from a tattered cross, hearing hymns filled with celestial superlatives, music unrelated to Jewish expression and culture, sermons denigrating Judaism, Aryan looking pictures of Jesus, statues of saints, worship of Mary, clerical collars, votive candles, nuns and priests, hell, fire and brimstone sermons, believers swooning in the aisles speaking in strange tongues and the presence of confessional booths. In light of this religious tossed salad, how can we tell the Jewish person "Christianity is Jewish"?

When the word *church* is used without any qualifiers in conversation with a Jewish non-believer, the Christian is to be sensitive to the message he or she may be unintentionally communicating.

Holy Ghost

This term is a carryover from the King James Bible's outdated rendering of *ghost* for the Greek *pneuma* instead of the more accurate English word *spirit*. Using this archaic language in a contemporary conversation will not draw the Jewish person any closer to an understanding of God as a tri-unity.

The word *ghost* adds a dimension of spookiness to our comprehension of God. After all, how does it sound to modern ears to be indwelt by a ghost - holy or not?

The Jewish scriptures refer to the *Holy Spirit* or *ruach ha-kodesh* as the *Spirit of the Lord*. In discussing the New Covenant concept of God, it is already difficult for a Jewish person to grasp the biblical nature of the plurality of God. Why throw in a term like *Holy Ghost* to muddy the waters even more for the seeking individual?

Section 5
Practices Missing in a Messianic Congregation

There is no need to provide a list of shoulds and should nots when it comes to fluency in messianic terminology. However, to maintain sensitivity to interested Jewish people, one will notice some missing elements in messianic settings.

Rather than questioning the spirituality of a messianic congregation and its leadership because of the lack of familiar cultural expressions, it may be more proper for the evangelical to question the basis for the inclusion of certain unbiblical Christian practices in local churches - the evangelical style of worship music, baptismal robes, church architecture, various procedures for distributing the elements of the Lord's Supper, ushers and other committees not mentioned in the scriptures, preferences for religious art and legalistic prohibitions against playing cards, viewing secular films and dancing. Not every practice found in a church is necessarily based on the Word of God, but has leaked into the Christian culture and eventually sanctioned.

Use of Traditional Christian Hymns

The discussion regarding the selection of contemporary praise songs versus traditional gospel hymns can fill several volumes. While a messianic congregation should not pass judgment on well-known and beloved hymns, it is common to observe the non-usage of these older song selections in a messianic fellowship.

The content of music is often selected for its ability to communicate biblical concepts and to sound more Jewish and contemporary in its rhythm and tempo. Some messianic ministries will only worship using messianic music while others also include contemporary praise songs in addition to Davidic dance to complement the worship.

When a Jewish person walks into a Christian setting, he or she is wondering if this atmosphere is going to harmonize with his or her own background. Though the traditional hymns contain classic melodies and deep theological truths, much of the music creates a "churchy" or "Gentile" atmosphere.

In addition, some hymns much loved in the Church carry negative connotations. A musical worship piece like "Onward Christian Soldiers" might sound like an evangelistic battle cry that can cause the Jewish person to start heading for the exit doors. Other hymns talk about the cross, the blood of Christ or other treasured Christian truths that are foreign and sometimes overpowering to Jewish ears because of negative historical connotations.

Unless the worship leader provides a context or background to these hymns, the seeker might feel uncomfortable having to dive into the classic truths of the Christian faith without having had too much exposure to evangelical teaching beforehand.

I have found that a great way to introduce the treasured hymns of the faith is for the worship band to use new musical arrangements along with the traditional melody.

When I entered the faith, I only heard traditional hymns and I grew to love many of them. However, I often felt the hymns were not used to worship God but to provide parishioners sentimental feelings much like I feel when I hear my favorite Oldie – But - Goodie Rock and Roll song. I enjoy the memories and emotions connected to a song even though the words mean nothing to me. The same experience often takes place in churches where Christians sing the words of these priceless hymns yet do not connect to the words but only to the emotions of singing "old favorites."

Altar Calls

In 1969 I prayed to receive Jesus as my Messiah and Lord. I was alone without any coaxing or anyone to force me to recite a sinner's prayer. I was deeply aware of my sins, the need to repent before a Holy God and fully cognizant of the eternal forgiveness Jesus offered me through His death on a Roman cross. I prayed to the best of my ability, confessing my sin and called out to Yeshua to save my soul. In that moment of repentance my life was transformed by the supernatural power of the Lord. Jesus was alive in my heart and I received Him as my Messiah and Redeemer.

After several months I attended a church service at which the pastor called people forward "to accept Christ into their lives by praying the sinner's prayer." He made the congregation feel unless one marches down the center church aisle in a public display of repentance, that person is not truly saved. I started to doubt my encounter with God and my salvation. I was confused and spoke to the minister.

I told the pastor I already prayed to ask Jesus into my life and had already experienced the might of the Lord to deliver me from major addictions I was struggling with. He insisted I pray once again. I refused knowing that walking down an aisle or "coming forward" is not what saves a person but rather the finished work of the Messiah. A few weeks later I was immersed in water and made a public statement to follow Yeshua.

What about the legitimacy of altar calls? Walking down an aisle to accept the Messiah is not rooted in the Bible but in evangelistic crusades during the Great Awakening revivals in the United States during the 1700s and 1800s. It is a practice reflective of Gentile Christian culture. Yet, it is a useful practice to make sure a person seeking salvation articulates his or her spiritual decision to another believer and publicly confesses their choice to become a child of God.

While most Jewish people may not feel comfortable enough to walk down a church aisle to accept Yeshua in front of an audience, other alternatives are acceptable. The pastor can ask for a show of hands on the part of those who pray to receive the Lord while the rest of the congregation is in reflective prayer; the leader can direct interested seekers to speak to him or any of the congregational staff or elders after the service to discuss spiritual matters and offer guidance to maintain accountability and begin a discipleship program of spiritual growth in the Christian life.

Again, the goal is not to embarrass the interested Jewish person nor to make him or her feel that walking down to the front of the congregation is what saves him. At the same time, public confession and acknowledgement is a must.

A personal, privatized relationship with the Lord is often the death knell for a growing, thriving faith that is active and serving in a body of believers. The Apostle Peter's letter impresses upon us the necessity for each congregational member to be visibly involved in serving the Lord: "Each one should use whatever gift he has received to serve others, faithfully administering God's grace in its various forms" (1 Peter 4:10).

Section 6
The Jewish People and All Their Holidays

Christians often remark there always seems to be another Jewish holiday on the horizon. In the fall Jewish people observe *Rosh Hashanah* (the New Year), *Yom Kippur* (Day of Atonement) and *Sukkoth* (Feast of Tabernacles).

In proximity to Christmas, Jewish people celebrate *Chanukah*. In the spring the major holidays are *Purim* (based on the Book of Esther), *Passover*, and *Shavuot* (Pentecost). Of course, there are other minor festivals like *Tisha B'Av*, *Lag B'Omer* and Israeli Independence Day.

Christians claim only two celebrations—Christmas and Easter. Yet if one surveys the denominations within Protestant Christianity and Roman Catholicism, the toll of Christian observances looms quite large: Maundy (Holy) Thursday; Lent, Pentecost, Advent season, Ash Wednesday, Epiphany, Christmas Eve, All Saint's Day, Palm Sunday, Good Friday, Assumption Day, Trinity Sunday, All Soul's Day and others. Count them up. Christianity wins by a large margin in the holiday competition.

In messianic congregations the practice of Christian holidays runs the full gamut. Some congregations refuse to acknowledge the existence of Christmas or Resurrection Day (Easter) while others observe messianized versions of these celebrations.

The danger in regard to these holidays occurs when a leader becomes judgmental and legalistic towards those who perform or fail to perform them, ignoring Paul's admonition, "Therefore do not let anyone judge you by what you eat or drink, or with regard to a religious festival, a New Moon celebration or a Sabbath day. These are a shadow of the things that were to come; the reality, however, is found in Christ" (Colossians 2:16-17).

Christmas

Rather than ignore this wonderful celebration, this day can be called "Celebration of Messiah's Birth" and honored in a congregational setting minus the Christmas trees and Santas. Instead of being party poopers and act disrespectfully toward fellow believers who celebrate Christmas, Jewish and Gentile followers of the Lord can use this season to declare our hope in the wonderful New Testament truth of the Incarnation of the Messiah.

Simeon, a devout Jew, who sought the coming of the Messiah declared upon seeing the newly born infant Jesus, "For my eyes have seen Your salvation, which You have prepared in the sight of all people, a light for revelation to the Gentiles and for glory to Your people Israel" (Luke 2:30-32). Can't believers do the same during the Christmas season instead of wearing the non-observance of Christmas as a badge of superiority as many Christians do?

Easter

The focus of this day is not on bunny rabbits and Easter eggs, but the resurrection of our Lord and Redeemer. In order to avoid the pagan ramifications of the name "Easter" and its connections with the false goddess *Ishtar*, worshipped as the "Queen of Heaven" in pagan cultures, the day can be renamed and reclaimed as "Resurrection Day." Jewish believers ought to join in a spirit of unity with Gentile believers and celebrate the resurrection of our Lord - the cardinal doctrine of our faith.

Section 7

If You Want to Trip Up a Jewish Seeker, Here's How

Wearing a Cross.

Christians have every right to wear crosses around their necks, display crosses in their sanctuaries and use them in Christian art and symbolism. In a messianic congregation, the display of the cross on a wall, a banner or flag can be considered insensitive. Remember, our aim is to have the Jewish person encounter a biblical understanding of the Messiah's death, not encounter a symbol he or she has not had the opportunity to understand.

The Jewish apostle Paul places the death of Jesus at the very center of his ministry: "For I resolved to know nothing while I was with you except Jesus Christ (Messiah) and him crucified" (I Corinthians 2:2). Paul also knew this message is offensive to Jewish people, "but we preach Christ (Messiah) crucified: a stumbling block to Jews and foolishness to Gentiles" (1 Corinthians 1:23).

But what was the stumbling block? A wooden cross around someone's neck? A bronze cross hanging over the baptistry? No. It is the **message of Jesus' death** that deals a blow to the pride and ego in recognizing the inability to save oneself and needing to turn to Jesus for eternal life through His death on the cross. This is the only display of the cross any non-believer should stumble over — not jewelry or symbols in a sanctuary. We want to make sure the Jewish person is stirred up by the message of God's redemptive love on the cross alone.

Should you wear a cross when in the presence of a Jewish person or at a messianic congregation? Ask yourself what is more important: The seeker hearing the message of God's love in the cross or being turned off by the glimmering crucifix around your neck? However, if you insist on wearing a cross and notice you're getting negative attention from a Jewish person, use this encounter as an opportunity to explain what the cross means to you.

Don't let the Jewish person draw his own conclusions about the cross around your neck, but provide that person with a biblical explanation of the wonderful story of the old rugged cross. Do all you can to diffuse the Jewish individual's false impressions of the cross gained from how it was distorted and misused throughout Christian history.

Other symbols like the *ichthus* (fish), the descending dove or other creative Christian jewelry do not carry the same cultural sting the cross delivers to the Jewish mindset. At the same time, as I said earlier in this booklet, it is time for Jewish believers in Yeshua who have been presented with the truth about the cross to restrain their overreaction to seeing the cross displayed and respond in a mature and respectful manner.

Display of Pictures of Jesus

Portraits of Jesus are a no-win situation. Most likenesses of Jesus depict Him as a golden-haired, fair-skinned ethereal man. Those daring artists who try to capture Jesus' Jewish nationality often go too far and accentuate non-flattering features like a large nose and wiry hair.

The Aryan, waspy non-Semitic look might work in major motion pictures about Jesus, but they do not capture His Semitic ethnicity. Then, there are those well-meaning artists who want to portray an African American Jesus or a Hispanic Jesus under the banner of universality. We are not sure what He looked like since the scriptures are silent on His physical description. We do know He was Jewish and not any other nationality.

The Samaritan woman in John 4 looked at Jesus and knew by His appearance or religious garb that He was Jewish. John 4:9 records, "The Samaritan woman said to him, "You are a Jew." His

Jewish lineage is also substantiated by the opening words of Matthew's gospel, "A record of the genealogy of Jesus Christ the son of David, the son of Abraham" (Matthew 1:1). Why would we want to display portraits of Jesus that are not reflective of His own first century lineage and nationality?

Can you blame Jewish people who are troubled by these pictures of Jesus? Christians believe Yeshua is the Son of God, and then try to portray images of Him in direct disobedience to the Scriptures: "You shall not make for yourself an idol in the form of anything in heaven above or on the earth beneath or in the waters below" (Exodus 20:4). Rather than present this man-made stumbling block of inaccurate portraits of Jesus, it is best to not adorn our sanctuaries with any pictorial depictions of what Jesus may have looked like.

Serving Non-Kosher Foods

Both Jewish and Gentiles followers of Jesus need maturity in this area. At congregational social events and potlucks where food is served, it is important not to blatantly serve non-kosher food like ham, bacon, pork chops or shrimp dishes. Often Gentile Christians might test a Jewish believer's "freedom from the Law" by seeing if he or she is willing to eat *traif* (non-kosher food).

Even if a messianic Jew chooses to remain kosher, it is not up to the Gentile Christian to purposely place a hurdle in his path. Romans 14:13-14 could not be clearer on this matter: "Therefore let us stop passing judgment on one another. Instead, make up your mind not to put any stumbling block or obstacle in your brother's way. As one who is in the Lord Jesus, I am fully convinced that no food is unclean in itself. But if anyone regards something as unclean, then for him it is unclean."

While believers are not to be judged by one another in their observance or non-observance of the Law of Moses, still many Jewish believers choose to express their Jewish heritage in observance of the biblical food laws. Romans 14:3 states, "The man who eats everything must not look down on him who does not, and the man who does not eat everything must not condemn the man who does, for God has accepted him."

On the matter of food laws Romans 14:17 provides the correct balance for Jewish and Gentile followers of Yeshua, "For the kingdom of God is not a matter of eating and drinking, but of righteousness, peace and joy in the Holy Spirit." The Jewish believer who decides to observe the biblical dietary restrictions must be confident ". . . that a man is not justified by observing the law, but by faith in Jesus Christ" (Galatians 2:16).

Likewise, Jewish believers are to be cautious not to shun fellowship with their Gentile brothers and sisters in the Lord because of the presence of non-kosher foods. The principle of the priority of "fellowship over food" comes into play (Romans 14:17). What good is it to pat yourself on the back for refraining from eating ham while isolating yourself from your fellow believers? Such a viewpoint belittles the work of the Messiah who reconciled Jews and Gentiles into one body (1 Corinthians 12:13; Ephesians 2:14-15) and places our adherence to food laws over and above the results of the finished ministry of the Messiah.

Section 8
Final Thoughts

It's a wrap. The guidelines offered in this book provide Christians clear cut principles on how to become fluent in messianic terms and thinking. If you are looking for a rationale for learning the messianic lingo, remember the words of Paul, "Though I am free and belong to no man, I make myself a slave to everyone, to win as many as possible. To the Jews, I became like a Jew, to win the Jews. To those under the law I became like one under the law (though I myself am not under the law), so as to win those under the law" (1 Corinthians 9:19-20).

Comedian Woody Allen once boasted, "I took a speed reading course and read 'War and Peace' in twenty minutes. It involves Russia." Anything learned too quickly usually doesn't stick, and it is harder to apply what is learned. To become sensitive to people seeking infinite truth takes an entire spiritual lifetime of learning and making mistakes. Familiarity with messianic jargon involves sensitivity in order to be God's instrument to present the good news of Israel's Messiah to Jewish people in an effective manner.

In "Yeshua or Jesus: Exploring the Jewish Roots of Christianity" Louis Lapides claims Jewish and Gentile followers of Christ can add a rich dimension to their Christian faith by understanding and employing messianic terms.

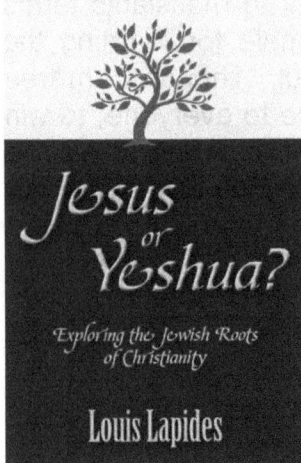

Lapides takes the reader on a tour of typical Christian lingo that can confuse newcomers to Christianity both Jewish and Gentile. His goal in compiling this guide is to help Gentile believers recognize certain "Christian" terms that have been historical stumbling blocks to Jewish seekers. In addition, Lapides aims to help Jewish people gain an appreciation for the deeper meaning of various Christian expressions.

This timely pamphlet will assist you in your search for a biblical and well-seasoned perspective that closes the gap for those who consider themselves at a distance from Christianity and better equip Christians to reach out to the Jewish community.

ABOUT LOUIS LAPIDES

As a Jewish follower of Jesus, Louis Lapides is equipped to address messianic issues. Louis earned graduate degrees in Old Testament Studies and taught in the Bible Department at BIOLA University. You can read more about Louis Lapides in the national best seller *The Case for Christ* and view his website at scripturesolutions.com

www.ingramcontent.com/pod-product-compliance
Lightning Source LLC
Chambersburg PA
CBHW060647030426
42337CB00018B/3485